How to Rate a Cat

Rate Any Feline Friend from Their Boopable Nose to Their Sweet Toe Beans

Matthew McGlasson

Social Media's No. 1 Cat Rater

ROCK POINT

Contents

The Cat Rating System (CRS)

Kittens

Adults

LET'S GET RATING!

Seniors

Fighters

The Cat Rating System (CRS)

Like most rating systems, the cat rating system is on a scale from 1 to 10, with 1 being the lowest score and 10 the highest. Unlike most rating systems, you are not allowed to rate a cat lower than 10, but you can go as high as you like. I know this doesn't make sense, but neither do cats, and that's what we love about them, right?!

There is no right or wrong way to rate a cat, as there's lots of criteria that can be judged, all subjective to the cat rater, of course. The best way to approach rating a cat is to not force it. What are the things that immediately stand out to you upon first seeing or meeting a feline friend?

The following pages include what I was looking for when rating the real-life cats (submitted by followers of my social media) featured in this book, along with a few surprises. I hope my ratings, which I must admit can be a bit absurd, not only make you laugh but also inspire you to become an expert cat rater!

Faces

SIZE
SHAPE
SMOOSHED
COLOR/MARKINGS
GRUMPY
JUDGYNESS

Eyes

SIZE
COLOR
EXPRESSIVENESS
GOOGLY-NESS
ASKEWNESS

Ears

SIZE
ALERTNESS
FOLDED
TORN/CLIPPED
FLOOFY
AIRPLANE

Teefs

FANGS
LITTLE CHOMPERS
TOOTHLESSNESS
SNAGGLERS

Noses

SIZE
COLOR
SHAPE
WETNESS FACTOR
SPECKLES
BOOPABLENESS

Moufs

SMOL
SMILING
EXPRESSIVENESS
FISHY BREFS
BIG YAWN CAPABILITY
BLEPPINESS

Chonkiness

SLEEK
SLIM
PETITE
PAUNCHY
AVERAGE
BIG BUDDY
OH LAWD,
THEY COMIN'!

Legs

ROCKETTE
SHORTIES
DRUMSTICKS
TATTOO FLEEVES

Peets

SMOL
SOCKS
POLYDACTYL
RABBIT-LIKE
CLICKETY-CLACKERS

Whiskers

NUMBER
LENGTH
TEXTURE
COLOR
POPPIN'

Bellies

(PRIMORDIAL POUCHES)

POOCHY
SOLID
FLOOFY
MARKINGS
TEMPERATURE

Floofiness

BUSHY
CLOSE-CROPPED
SILKY
TEXTURED
HAIRLESS
CHESTS/BIBS
BED BODY

LENGTH
FLOOFY
NUBBY
STRAIGHT
CURLY
SQUIRRELY

Tails

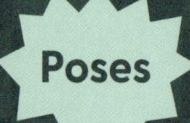

Poses

SO REGAL
LOAF OF BREAD
LITTLE BUN
BIG STRETCHER
PET THIS BELLY
EMO (HUNCHED OVER)
BEST SLEEPER

Purrsonality

LOVER
SWEETEST
ANGEL
SNOOGLER
SUPER
SILLIEST
WEIRDO
COOL CAT
CRANKY

Catitude

THAT *JE NE*
SAIS QUOI

Vocalness

CHATTINESS
MEWS
MEEPS
MRRPS
CRYBABIES
SCREAMERS

Color/Markings

STRIPES
SWIRLS
PATCHES
TUXEDOS
SPOTS
MITTENS
RECOGNIZABLE SHAPES

Skillz

TRICKS
GOOD PLAYER
HUNTER
HELPER
CLEANEST
CARDBOARD BOX INSPECTOR

LET'S GET RATING!

Kittens

0-TO-3-YEAR-OLDS

Violet

About

Violet is a rare mix of a potato and a lion. She carries everything around in her mouth and often puts her favorite toys in her food dish.

LOCATION

Summerville, South Carolina

GENDER

Female

AGE

0.5

TYPE

British shorthair and domestic longhair (beige)

FLOOFINESS

25/10

Violet knows how to rock some bed body.

EARS/WHISKERS
It's a battle of the ear floofs vs. the whiskers. 34/10

26/10 **POSE**
So young, yet so regal.

MOUF

35/10

It's so serious for such a little bebe.

CHONKINESS
There's definitely a solid potato under all that fur. 50/10

Felix

LOCATION
Halifax, Nova Scotia

GENDER
Male

AGE
1

TYPE
Domestic shorthair
(brown tabby)

About

Felix has a smooshed face and a crispy tongue, and is the most distinguished little man.

MOUF

40/10

When you are noted for your "crispy tongue," the blep (sticking your tongue out) factor is gonna be high.

FACE

45/10

Felix is tired of hearing all your sad stories because of his CEX (Concerned Expression Factor). *See also* Face.

PURRSONALITY

80/10

Felix's "distinguished little man" persona is pretty maxed out, though he could up it even further with the addition of a monocle, top hat, and cane.

CATITUDE

100/10

"I know you want to aggressively kiss this smooshy face, but don't even think about it . . ."

FACE

75/10

First impressions are tough when you have RSF (Resting Squish Face). *See also* Face.

Lumi and Hinoki

CATITUDE

88/10

"We hungry girls and we proud of it!"

LOCATION

Buffalo, New York

GENDER

Female

AGE

1

TYPE

Maine Coon
(Lumi: black silver tabby
Hinoki: blue tabby,
polydactyl)

About

Lumi and Hinoki are littermates and the yin to the other's yang. They love to play fetch like a dog and are so passionate about food that when they are eating, you can hear them purring from the floor below.

VOCALNESS

Their diesel-engine purrs cause the whole house to shake.

89/10

PURRSONALITY

Their yin and yangness make them purrfectly complementary, sweet little ladies.

76/10

PEETS

87/10

You never know when you might need one of Hinoki's spare beans.

SKILLZ

68/10

How can we put those fetching skillz to good use?

Jack

LOCATION

Yardley, Pennsylvania

GENDER

Male

AGE

1

TYPE

Domestic shorthair (orange tabby with white)

About

Just look at the way he sits!

COLOR

45/10

He's the purrfect orangy-ness. I hear Pantone is about to intoduce a new color called Jack.

EARS

50/10

Jack's Doritos ears have all the nacho-cheese goodness without the Doritos dust.

35/10

PEETS

Jack doesn't care what Gen Z thinks about his teeny white socks.

CATITUDE

74/10

"Come sit on my lap and tell me what you'd like for Christmas. Have you been a good little kitten this year?"

100/10

POSE
The way he
sits. Come on!
Stop it!

Xavier

LOCATION
Strathroy, Ontario

GENDER
Male

AGE
1.5

TYPE
Siamese
(lynx point)

About

Xavier was a foster fail. We just couldn't imagine our lives without him. He always seems a bit off, but that makes him our little weirdo. He looks at us with those big blue eyes, saying, "FOOD?"

47/10 CATITUDE
"FOOOOOOOD?!"

EYES
50/10
One look and you're transported to the ocean. Surf's up!

NOSE
41/10
Only an expert cat rater can get past those ocean eyes and see the beauty of that tricolor nose!

FLOOFINESS
55/10
When your catitude is "food," you need to have a nice big bebe bib.

BEING A NORMAL CAT IS OVERRATED ... AND BORING!

PURRSONALITY **60/10**
Xavier is a "little weirdo" in a good way, of course.

Yzma

LOCATION
Gillsville, Georgia

GENDER
Female

AGE
2

TYPE
Sphynx (mink)

About

Yzma keeps her slim figure even with an abundant appetite. She likes to challenge everyone to eating contests and will sometimes try to finish your food before you have a chance to. She also helps with household chores, especially laundry. She knows when the dryer is finished and then jumps right in to help.

CHONKINESS
78/10
Yzma was truly made for the catwalk with that slinky figure.

SKILLZ
20/10
Being a good helper, especially with laundry? What a dream!

PURRSONALITY
55/10
"If you're not gonna finish your food, Mom, I'd hate for it to go to waste." Such a thoughtful kitty, and so concerned about food waste!

COLOR
50/10
The rotisserie chicken factor is high with Yzma. I repeat: do not take her to Costco, where hungry people are lining up for those chickens.

FLOOFINESS
85/10
No retinol is needed for her purrfect wrinkliness.

Freddie Purr-curry

About

Freddie Purr-curry was a stray who was screaming in the bushes next to my house. He is a lovable, always-purring baby who loves to be held.

LOCATION

Bedford, Ohio

GENDER

Male

AGE

2

TYPE

Domestic longhair
(black tuxedo)

VOCALNESS

76/10

Screaming for attention is one way to get adopted.

FLOOFINESS

40/10

This is I-want-to-rub-my-face-in-that-belly floofiness!

FACE

90/10

This mustache will "rock you ... (rock you)."

FACE

60/10

Freddie Purr-curry couldn't just have a cool '70s stache ... he also has a beard.

PURRSONALITY

The hold-me-I-just-a-bebe factor really hits.

39/10

Emma

LOCATION

Brooklyn, New York

GENDER

Female

AGE

2

TYPE

Domestic shorthair
(brown tabby
with white)

About

Emma is a petite princess who is practically perfect in every way.

MARKINGS

45/10

The tabby symmetry is purrfect, from head to peets.

EMMA CLEARLY KEEPS HER EMOTIONS ON THE INSIDE.

LEGS
89/10

"Yes, I have tattoo fleeves I am from Brooklyn."

CATITUDE

88/10

"I'm still in my emo phase. Is my eyeliner smudged?"

MOUF

61/10

You're going to have to work hard to get Emma to crack a smile.

PURRSONALITY
57/10

Try saying "practically perfect petite princess" three times in a row.

Buddy "The Elf" Edens

LOCATION
Houston, Texas

GENDER
Male

AGE
2

TYPE
Possibly Siamese and Himalayan (seal point)

About
Buddy is a happy, chirpy boy. He has a magnificent squirrelly tail that he waves proudly as he runs all over the house and beautiful owl-like eyes that have won many staring contests. Buddy loves everyone, and everyone loves him. How could they not?!

PEETS
49/10
Sometimes the occasion calls for dark socks. Just don't pair them with sandals.

EARS/WHISKERS
30/10
I've never seen such purrfect ear floof and whisker symmetry!

77/10
VOCALNESS
I'm starting to think Buddy isn't a cat at all . . . not only does he have a squirrel tail and owl eyes, but he also chirps.

Newton (Newt)

LOCATION

Chicago, Illinois

GENDER

Male

AGE

2

TYPE

Domestic shorthair
(black and white)

About

Newt is the babiest man and looooves to cuddle with his sisters and mommy more than anything, except hunting bugs. He has the cutest peets with speckles and tiny beans that are meticulously maintained while perched on his daddy's lap.

99/10

NOSE

Newt has the purrfect ink-blot nose. What would Rorschach see?

SKILLZ

88/10

High marks for being a multitasker! He can clean his peets and be a lap warmer at the same time.

72/10

PURRSONALITY

Newt's a cuddle bug who hunts bugs. Awww!

SKILLZ

44/10

He's such a good bug hunter that you don't need to pay for an exterminator. Nice!

PEETS

66/10

Those speckled peets are almost good enough to eat, like chocolate chip ice cream.

Chrissie

LOCATION

Maple Grove, Minnesota

GENDER

Female

AGE

3

TYPE

Domestic shorthair (calico)

About

A tough little survivor of the stray life, Chrissie was found in the "middle of the road" and named after Chrissie Hynde of The Pretenders. A big fan of the sink, the sun, and The Snacks, she brings unending joy, exuberance, and love to our family (which includes four other rescue cats).

MARKINGS

77/10

If you have been wondering what the difference is between a calico, tortoiseshell, and torbie, Chrissie has purrfect calico markings.

NOSE

58/10

Chrissie's pink nose is highly boopable. Boop! Bop!

PEETS

91/10

Her mixed calico beans are like a three bean salad. Protein!

WHISKERS

39/10

Those eyebrow whiskers are poppin'!

PURRSONALITY

Chrissie will always "stand (or sit, or lie) by you."

99/10

"DON'T GET ME WRONG," RIGHT? (OKAY, I'LL STOP NOW.)

LOCATION

Fort Wright, Kentucky

GENDER

Female

AGE

3

TYPE

Domestic shorthair
(black with a little white)

Bella

About

Bella is a silly girl with one white armpit. Her stomach is white as well, but she is black everywhere else. She loves to lick people all over.

BEANS/NOSE

89/10

Bella has purrfect coordination with her black beans and nose

TEEFS

67/10

Bella has some sharp little vampire chompers.

SKILLZ

50/10

All over licky-ness is definitely special. Let's just hope that kitty brefs is fresh!

COLOR

666/10

VOID.

FLOOFINESS

44/10

White armpit floof is always adorable, unlike when white deodorant gets on a black shirt. Hate that!

Chester

LOCATION
San Diego, California

GENDER
Male

AGE
3

TYPE
Siamese (flame point)

About

Chester was found roaming around Tijuana, Mexico, as a stray kitten. He had multiple health problems, including a hernia and an undescended testicle, and he was malnourished. Now he is the happiest, smartest, most jovial cat you'll ever meet.

88/10

COLOR/
MARKINGS
Purrfect Siameseyness.

EARS
55/10

So alert and probably a great listener too.

NOSE

39/10

That pink nose is begging for a boop.

VOCALNESS

78/10

Chester can meow in English and Spanish.

MIAO! (ENGLISH TRANSLATION: MEOW!)

PURRSONALITY
Chester is the nicest and smartest boi.

49/10

Luna

LOCATION

Celina, Texas

GENDER

Female

AGE

3

TYPE

Russian Blue mix (gray)

COLOR

55/10

Her fur has the shimmer, glitter, and sparkle factor. She's a feline disco ball!

About

Luna is a very anxious stunner. She hates the doorbell, loud sneezes, and the mini vacuum. However, she is very funny and spunky with a sassy sense of humor. She likes to play fetch, supervise the human's chores, and chitchat.

SKILLZ

78/10

"Quiet pleeze…" Luna would make a great librarian.

VOCALNESS

34/10

I can't confirm myself, but I'm feeling confident on this chitchattiness rating.

MOUF

27/10

Luna's got a smiliness factor thanks to her extra-wide mouf.

PURRSONALITY

30/10

She's the purrfect little elegant lady.

Taffy the Boardwalk Cat

LOCATION

Haddonfield, New Jersey

GENDER

Female

AGE

3

TYPE

Domestic shorthair ("harlequin," white with tabby splotches)

About

Taffy had a hard-luck beginning at the Jersey Shore, but she's in good hands now. She rates 1,000 out of 10 for being splattered with tabby.

MARKINGS

$105/10$

I guess if you have a paintbrush tail, you end up with adorable tabby splatters!

VOCALNESS

$39/10$

Of course she meows with a Jersey accent. Born and bred!

$47/10$

PURRSONALITY

I reckon Taffy is as sweet as saltwater taffy.

42

TAIL
34/10

Taffy has a tail that looks like it has been dipped in white paint.

CATITUDE
Watch out, Snooki! There's a new Jersey Girl in town.

88/10

LET'S GET RATING!

Adults

4-TO-9-YEAR-OLDS

Saffron

LOCATION
Columbus, Ohio

GENDER
Female

AGE
4

TYPE
Domestic shorthair
(gray tuxedo)

About
Saffron is highly expressive and intelligent! She loves to Peloton with me, hanging out on the handlebars or my shoulders, but she tires quickly and then stares at me like she can't wait to be done with our workout.

74/10

SKILLZ
It's always good to have a motivational workout partner and coach!

46

CATITUDE

39/10

"I think we've worked out long enough, Mom."

FACE

88/10

Ooh, that's the softest, whitest chin. It needs some scratchies!

EYES

38/10

Saffon's eyes have just the right amount of googly-ness. Can I buy sticker versions of them?

76/10

PURRSONALITY

Just like the spice, Saffron is extra special.

47

LOCATION

Cashion, Oklahoma

GENDER

Male

AGE

4

TYPE

Domestic shorthair
(red point with white)

Brunswick

About

Brunswick is so loving to us and intimidating to our other cats. His crossed eyes are just too cute to be ignored.

PURRSONALITY
77/10
Brunswick is the goodest boi. Ever.

NOSE
553/10
He has the sweetest black nose speckles! No wonder he's always looking down at it.

TAIL
89/10
Love that instant-ramen-noodle tail. Slurp!

EYES
564/10
Brunswick has the bestest, sweetest crossed eyes.

CATITUDE
"Don't fluff with me!"
99/10

LOCATION
Omaha, Nebraska
GENDER
Female
AGE
5
TYPE
Ragdoll (seal mitted mink, brown and white)

Princess Leia

About

Princess Leia's a sassy pants who talks, trills, and meows all in one sentence. She has major catitude and fur like a mink coat, with back legs that look like she's walking in high heels.

COLOR/MARKINGS
65/10
Purrfect Ragdolliness.

CATITUDE
49/10
"If you think I'm sassy, you should see my pants."

PEETS
55/10
These boots are made fur walkin'.

VOCALNESS
57/10
Princess Leia has a secret kitty dialect.

A GREAT SKILL TO HAVE WHEN YOU NEED TO COMMUNICATE WITH JABBA THE HUTT.

FLOOFINESS
Mink coat (PETA approved).
78/10

Pinky

LOCATION
San Francisco, California

GENDER
Male

AGE
5

TYPE
Domestic shorthair (orange tabby with white)

52

About

With his fluffy white tummy, pink beans, and clipped ear, Pinky's one handsome dude.

66/10

COLOR
Pinky gets a high rating for being an orange bebe lion.

NOSE

48/10

If you look very closely, you'll see some tiny black nose speckles.

BEANS

92/10

Perhaps Pinky's named after those stunning pink beans of his?

39/10

EARS
That clipped ear is pretty bada**.

PURRSONALITY
Pinky is the chillest boi. Must be that California lifestyle.

53/10

Milo Huckleberry Ventimiglio

LOCATION
Toronto, Ontario

GENDER
Male

AGE
5

TYPE
Domestic shorthair (silver tabby)

About
Milo is a total people person. He's super affectionate and a total attention seeker. He does a "faint" flop to encourage petting, but don't touch his belly unless you'd like your hand and arm to be eviscerated.

POSE
27/10

Milo is a natural lounger, making himself comfortable anywhere.

FLOOFINESS
38/10

Milo's chest floofs rival an Elizabethan ruff.

88/10

EARS

Though it's subtle, his ear notch is super cool.

LEGS

67/10

Speaking of cool, Milo has tattoo fleeves.

MOUF

48/10

"Who needs hand sanitizer when you have tongue like dis?"

Bean

LOCATION
Mesa, Arizona

GENDER
Female

AGE
6

TYPE
Domestic shorthair (half-dilute calico)

About
Bean is an ear-tipped former feral who came for dinner as usual one day and then never left. She is a sweet, chatty, chinchilla-soft angel baby who has never done anything wrong. Ever.

PURRSONALITY
99/10
Bean's never done anything wrong and must really be an angel baby. AH-MAHZING!

NOSE
77/10
What a purrfect snow-capped mountain!

63/10
FLOOFINESS
Chinchilla fur is highly sought-after, so watch your back, Bean!

VOCALNESS

46/10

"Listen hooman,
I talkin'."

COLOR/
MARKINGS

56/10

She likes to
keep her calico
on the DL.

Ozzie

LOCATION

Wilton, Maine

GENDER

Male

AGE

6

TYPE

Maine Coon (silver)

About

Ozzie has helped me foster and socialize several litters of feral kittens that come to me from the shelter without their mamas. He tends to them just like a mama, and even goes so far as to let them "nurse." Without him, some of the ferals would never have been socialized enough to be adopted. He is their ambassador to trust humans.

FLOOFINESS
93/10
I'd love a shag rug as fuzzy as Ozzie.

BELLY
55/10
The purrfect primordial pouch to rest one's weary head.

SKILLZ
98/10
Best. Foster. Dad. Ever.

CATITUDE
44/10
"I love all the kitties."

PURRSONALITY
78/10
He's a silver boi with a heart of gold.

Ganymede

LOCATION

Victoria, British Columbia

GENDER

Female

AGE

6

TYPE

Burmese (platinum)

About

Ganymede has a smoker's hoarse warble instead of a meow. She also doesn't know how to groom herself and just kind of gets damp instead.

FACE

43/10

Does having a grumpy face make for a grumpy cat? Something to think about.

VOCALNESS

77/10

I can definitely hear her scratchy meow in my head.

FLOOFINESS

48/10

Ganymede's floofiness may be a side effect of not being able to groom properly. Anyway, it's working for her!

POSE

84/10

"Is this how you position your legs to 'clean' oneself?"

68/10

CATITUDE

"I don't care if you can see my butt."

Angel

LOCATION

Oklahoma City, Oklahoma

GENDER

Male

AGE

6

TYPE

Domestic shorthair (chocolate brown tabby mix)

PURRSONALITY

His goodest boi factor is off the charts.

79/10

About

Angel loves cuddles and belly rubs and does tricks like giving high fives and handshakes. He also knows when someone is anxious or sad and will try to make them feel better.

BELLY
63/10

I'm seeing a hairy chest there.

CHONKINESS

78/10

Angel is what I'd call a "big buddy."

SKILLZ

99/10

High fives all around for this guy!

CATITUDE

88/10 Angel is a serotonin dispenser. Who wouldn't want him to cheer them up?

Muffin

LOCATION
London, England

GENDER
Female

AGE
7

TYPE
Domestic shorthair
(brown mackerel tabby)

About

Muffin makes soothing purring sounds while she sleeps between my legs, uses a gentle paw tap to wake me up every morning at 5:30, and greets me at the door when I come home. She's my furry daughter!

PURRSONALITY
48/10
Muffin just has "it," that cool factor.

FACE
68/10
Though Muffin is an adult, she has the face of a lil' bebe.

EYES
88/10
Those expressive anime eyes!

PEETS
37/10
Muffin's smol peets are an architectural marvel holding up her upper body and head.

NOW I UNDERSTAND MUFFIN'S CONCERNED FACE. SHE HAS A LOT OF RESPONSIBILITIES.

SKILLZ
88/10
She's a calming sound machine and an alarm clock.

Skye Blue Humphrey Bogart (Bogie)

LOCATION
St. Joseph, Minnesota

GENDER
Male

AGE
7

TYPE
Siberian (calico point)

About
Bogie is a rare male calico point with blue eyes. He has a sweet, friendly temperament and is very intelligent.

COLOR/ MARKINGS
199/10

For being a rare calico boi.

45/10

FACE
You must admire those Lorax cheeks.

161/10

SKILLZ
I'm pretty sure Bogie has an IQ of 161 and is a Mensa member.

EYES

57/10

Ol' Blue Eyes.
Oh, wait, that's
Frank Sinatra.

FLOOFINESS 44/10
Threat-level floof goblin.

Brandi

About

When I adopted Brandi from the shelter six months ago, she was a morbidly obese and traumatized mess of a cat, who weighed 22 pounds (10 kg) and had undergone multiple surgeries due to health issues. We bonded almost immediately, and after a few months of dieting and medication, she's now my happy and healthy best friend!

LOCATION
Pittsburgh, Pennsylvania

GENDER
Female

AGE
7

TYPE
Domestic shorthair
(gray and white)

SKILLZ
68/10

Brandi's determination to stick to her diet is to be applauded!

SPOKESCAT POTENTIAL IS HIGH WITH THIS ONE. SHE'S THE TOTAL PACKAGE!

BELLY
47/10
Such a squishy tummy! I want to squeeze it like one of those stress-relief balls.

NOSE
58/10

Brandi's smudged nose is just the smudgiest.

CATITUDE
39/10

"If I can do it, you can do it."

79/10

PURRSONALITY
Purrfectness!

Rashida Leopards (Zoey)

LOCATION
Niles, Michigan

GENDER
Female

AGE
8

TYPE
Domestic shorthair (torbie)

About
I rescued Miss Zoey around six years ago, and she hasn't stopped talking since. She wants nothing more than to follow me around and talk the whole time. Oh, the conversations we have!

SKILLZ
58/10

Zoey is so good at being Mommy's shadow.

EARS
66/10

They look like little slices of pizza. Nom nom!

93/10 PURRSONALITY
Zoey is the sweetest, most grateful rescue kitty.

VOCALNESS

87/10

Everyone loves a good gossip queen.

"DID YOU HEAR THAT HELLO KITTY ISN'T A CAT BUT A LITTLE GIRL?!"

56/10

COLOR/ MARKINGS
Extra-special torbieness.

Carmine

LOCATION
Boca Raton, Florida

GENDER
Male

AGE
9

TYPE
Bengal (brown)

About
Carmine has a twin sister, and they're both sweet, clever, snuggly, and love to go for runs. Plus, they are toilet-trained!

55/10

MOUF
His black lipstick is so goth! *See also* Eyes.

MARKINGS

45/10

Carmine's accessorizing is fabulous. I see necklaces, and you can never go wrong with a leopard print.

EYES

68/10

The purrfect eyeliner to go with that black lipstick. Cue The Cure! *See also* Mouf.

SKILLZ

97/10

Being able to use the toilet is up there.

BUT CAN HE FLUSH?

CATITUDE

75/10

"I was born to run."

Simba

LOCATION
Bucharest, Romania

GENDER
Male

AGE
9

TYPE
Mixed British shorthair (beige)

CHONKINESS
56/10
Such a roly-poly. I want to give him a big hug.

About
Simba gets mad when he has to see the vet! Nothing bad ever happens there, but it just makes him mad. He stays cranky the entire day, and it's the only time I ever hear him hiss and growl.

PEETS

49/10

Big peets, not to be confused with Bigfoot.

87/10 EYES

Simba's amber eyes look like beautiful fossils.

66/10

MOUF

Simba's Elvis Presley lip is saying, "Thank you, thank you very much."

95/10 PURRSONALITY

As a vet, I allow this crankiness!

LET'S GET RATING!

Seniors

10-TO-24.5-YEAR-OLDS

Caramel

LOCATION
Burnaby,
British Columbia

GENDER
Male

AGE
10

TYPE
Domestic Longhair
(ginger/caramel)

About

Caramel is extra special because he is a fluffy purr machine who is always there for me.

PURRSONALITY

49/10

Caramel is as sweet as his name. Awww!

LEGS

67/10

They're shorties but cuties.

CATITUDE

88/10

"Mom, I right here!"

VOCALNESS

87/10

We've got a 200 catpower purr machine here.

FLOOFINESS

Caramel could definitely join ZZ Top.

73/10

Little T

LOCATION
New York, New York

GENDER
Female

AGE
10

TYPE
Domestic shorthair (black tuxedo)

About
Little T lives in a studio apartment where she obviously rules the roost. When she isn't being harassed by the birdies on the fire escape, she likes to play with her many toys, get bathroom sink drinks, and wake up her dad multiple times a night to get freshies (fresh food) and scratchies.

12/10

LEGS
As you can see, Little T is very fashionable, especially her knee-high white socks.

NOSE
35/10
Little T has a purrfect black nose that is highly boopable.

POSE
25/10
She is exhibiting a classic "I dare you to touch my belly" pose.

CATITUDE
"When I'm awake, you're awake."
50/10

DO NOT, I REPEAT, DO NOT FALL FOR THIS CLASSIC CAT TRAP!!!

FACE
Her expression shows a high level of judgyness: "Yes, I know I'm adorable."
17/10

Dave

LOCATION
Ajijic, Mexico

GENDER
Male

AGE
13

TYPE
Sphynx (pink)

About

Oh, Dave ... what can I say about him? He's a dork. He loves paper, so we had to put Dave Doors in our bathrooms to protect the toilet paper.

COLOR/FLOOFINESS

94/10

Dave is the purrfect combo of bebe and oldie with that pink-yet-wrinkly skin.

CHONKINESS

39/10

Dave could be mistaken for a nice-size raw chicken. Be careful, Dave!

EARS

88/10

"I'm receiving a signal ... "

CATITUDE

75/10

"I will get that toilet paper no matter what. Dave Doors can't stop me!"

PURRSONALITY

87/10

"You may think I'm a dork, but you just don't understand that there's an alien in your midst." *See also* Ears.

Marco

LOCATION

Victoria,
British Columbia

GENDER

Male

AGE

13

TYPE

Domestic shorthair
(white)

About

An hour after Marco was adopted,
he was napping within arm's reach,
and has slept curled into my chest
at night ever since (since 2020)! He's
very chatty and can transform himself
from a senior cat to a tiny baby kitten
with a well-selected mew.

CATITUDE
High marks for the
old man–bebe factor.

88/10

97/10

COLOR/ FLOOFINESS
Just the whitest, fluffiest cloud. I see a cat!

VOCALNESS
89/10
No one can resist smol mews.

BELLY
64/10
"It's okay, you can touch my floofy tummy."

SKILLZ
78/10
Marco's a natural weighted blankie for his hooman.

CJ and Coco

About

Coco was the peanut of her litter, and CJ was the
big boy. CJ is a quiet, shy lover boy, and teeny Coco
is the mouthy supervisor of everything in the house.
They like to sleep curled up into one big ball.

LOCATION
Wading River, New York

GENDER
Male/Female

AGE
14

TYPE
Domestic shorthair
(black tuxedo)

CATITUDE
99/10
"We are the poster cats for adopting bonded pairs."

SKILLZ
96/10
They are the very best sibling snooglers.

PURRSONALITY
98/10
Coco is the yin to CJ's yang. Or is CJ the yin to Coco's yang?

"WE ARE NOT IDENTICAL TWINS."
—Julius Benedict, *Twins*

WHISKERS
77/10
There's no doubt they're siblings with those matching poppin' whiskers.

89/10

POSE
Are you seeing Arnold Schwarzenegger and Danny DeVito in *Twins*, or is it just me?

Bubbles

LOCATION
Portland, Oregon

GENDER
Female

AGE
15

TYPE
Domestic medium hair (white)

POSE
78/10

Just make yourself comfortable.

About

Bubbles's favorite food is bread, but not just any bread. She wants high-quality French bread or croissants.

SKILLZ

77/10

"I eat loaf and I can be loaf."

VOCALNESS

89/10

She can meow in French and say, "Je voudrais un croissant, s'il vous plaît."

PURRSONALITY

47/10

Bubbles is the sweetest girl who deserves the finest things in life.

CATITUDE / COLOR

88/10

If Bubbles was a hooman, her name would be Blanche.

Romeo (MoMo)

LOCATION
Raleigh, North Carolina

GENDER
Male

AGE
15

TYPE
Ragdoll (blue bicolor)

About

MoMo loves to "tuck and roll" for belly rubs from his favorite people and groom his humans' freshly washed wet hair.

FLOOFINESS
38/10
Purrfect grandpa-bebe floofiness.

FACE
53/10
If anyone can pull off a bucket hat, it's Romeo.

PURRSONALITY
67/10
Born to be a hair stylist.

POSE
10/10
This tuck-and-roll gymnast gets a purrfect score from the judges.

SKILLZ
99/10
"No need for hairbrush, hooman. Try my tongue instead."

Edie

LOCATION
Tremont, Illinois

GENDER
Female

AGE
15

TYPE
Domestic shorthair
(calico)

About

Edie is literally the biggest sweetheart you'll ever meet. She's not much of a lap cat, but she sure loves getting pets on the kitchen table. And despite that girth, she can still jump up on the table to get those pets!

SKILLZ

55/10

Hot take: Pets on the table? Yes, pleeze.

FACE

97/10

Purrfect calico symmetry.

LEGS

66/10

Those little legs are working overtime.

CHONKINESS

78/10

OH LAWD! SHE COMIN'!!

PURRSONALITY

Such a sweet, lovely granny overall.

77/10

Tuesday

LOCATION
Fort Wayne,
Indiana

GENDER
Female

AGE
17

TYPE
Domestic shorthair
(black)

About

Tuesday enjoys taking walks with me (she's leash-trained). She's absolutely great with people, will let anyone pet her, and is really good at the vet (though she hisses at someone at least once a visit; otherwise, she will let them do whatever).

COLOR

77/10

The senior void is strong with this one.

95/10

PURRSONALITY
A purrfect old lady every day of the week.

SKILLZ

88/10

Whether Mom is walking Tuesday, or Tuesday is walking Mom, the leash training is impressive.

BWGE (BIG WALMART GREETER ENERGY) WITH THIS ONE.

CATITUDE

88/10

"Oh, hi!"

FLOOFINESS
Her furriendliness is apparent, as her fur looks ruffled from all the pets she must get on those walks.

49/10

Los Angeles, California

GENDER

Female

AGE

18

TYPE

Domestic shorthair (gray and white)

Pepper

About

Pepper is by far the sweetest cat I've ever known and a major Velcro cat. Plus, her white-tipped tail is adorable.

78/10

TAIL

The white tip of that fluffy tail could poke me in the eye any day.

PURRSONALITY 87/10
I'm not just saying this out of respect to my elders. Pepper is a real sweet lady.

SKILLZ 99/10
Don't we all wish our cats were Velcro cats? So lucky!

VELCRO CAN ALSO COME IN HANDY FOR THIS SENIOR CAT. →

COLOR 88/10
Pepper can finally embrace her cool gray-and-white granny vibe in her golden years.

BELLY 46/10
She is really owning her poochy tummy.

Neesha

LOCATION

Missoula, Montana

GENDER

Female

AGE

19

TYPE

Domestic shorthair,
Maine Coon, Persian,
and Russian Blue
(gray)

About

Neesha has extra toes and beautiful two-toned green eyes and is a very old lady. She can also sense her mom's seizures.

99/10

PURRSONALITY
Is she a granny or a kitty? I say she's a lil' granny kitty!

EYES
69/10

When you look up "cat eyes" in the encyclopedia, there's a picture of Neesha's purrfect eyes.

PEETS
99/10

She has special mittens to comfort her mommy.

SKILLZ
99/10

Neesha is the sweetest angel who takes the very best care of her mom.

SUCH A SPECIAL CAT WHO CAN SENSE SEIZURES!

COLOR
Being a gray cat, Neesha has always had the spirit of an older lady.

67/10

Rex

About

In the nineteen-plus years I've had Rex, he's won over a ton of "I don't like cats" people with his sweet and sassy personality. Several of them have gotten their own cats—probably not coincidently, orange ones.

LOCATION

Westford, Vermont

GENDER

Male

AGE

19

TYPE

Domestic shorthair
(orange tabby)

COLOR

98/10

Some old men turn gray and others turn rusty, like this purrfect orange gramps.

NO WD-40 IS NEEDED FOR THIS RUSTY FELLOW. JUST LOOK AT THAT SLEEPING FORM (OPPOSITE).

EARS

79/10

I just want to crunch and munch on those Doritos ears.

44/10

CATITUDE

"Have you read *How to Win Friends and Influence People* by Dale Carnegie?"

SKILLZ

78/10

"You hate cats? Great. Let me just slt on your lap for a bit."

85/10

PURRSONALITY

If Rex were a human, he would eat the same breakfast at the same restaurant at the same time every morning.

Selma

LOCATION

Cincinnati, Ohio

GENDER

Female

AGE

20

TYPE

Domestic Longhair
(brown marble)

About

Selma is a young twenty years old, and like Sally O'Malley, played by Molly Shannon on *Saturday Night Live*, she still likes to stretch and kick! She was born on the cold streets of Chicago, and along with her sister, Patty, they have not only managed to survive but also delight everyone they meet.

78/10

POSE

You can't kick unless you do your daily stretches.

46/10

WHISKERS
There are whiskers, and then there are old-lady whiskers.

CATITUDE

99/10

"I'm a queen who lives in the Queen City."

VOCALNESS

99/10

"I'm 20! 20 years old," said in Sally O'Malley's voice.

PURRSONALITY
60/10

Selma and her sister, Patty, really do seem like the cat versions of their namesakes, Marge Simpson's sisters.

Pepperricka (Pepper)

LOCATION

Midvale, Utah

GENDER

Male

AGE

22

TYPE

Domestic shorthair (gray tabby with white)

POSE
Pepper is always purrfectly positioned to take a cat nap.

About

Pepperricka was named after baby Paprika from *Blue's Clues* by his bubber (human brother) when they were both three. Now they are both twenty-two.

MOUF

48/10

I thought body parts grew as we aged, but not that smol mouf.

NOSE

40/10

Pepper's highly boopable nose purrfectly complements his smol mouf.

CATITUDE

99/10

"When I was your age, I walked to the litter box uphill both ways."

CHONKINESS

97/10

Pepper's chonkiness is well earned, making him a big healthy boi.

China

LOCATION

Williamsburg,
Massachusetts

GENDER

Female

AGE

24.5

TYPE

Domestic shorthair
(black and white)

78/10

It's the purrfect
flat shape to
set things on.
Hold my drink!

About

China is super sassy
and has so much
spirit/will to live.
Although she's
slightly blind and
half deaf, she runs
the household with
an iron paw.

COLOR/ MARKINGS

99/10

China is the sweetest cat-cow granny. "Mooeow!"

MAY WE ALL BE SO LUCKY TO HAVE A CAT WHO LIVES THIS LONG. A STANDING OVATION FOR CHINA!
↓

PURRSONALITY

89/10

"Has anyone seen my cat-eye glasses?"

CATITUDE

95/10

"I'm 95 in hooman years. I'm the oldest cat in this book, and I can do whatever I pleeze."

LEGS

58/10

What sides do we have to go with those drumsticks?

LET'S GET RATING!

Fighters

ALL AGES

Pippin

LOCATION
St. Cloud, Minnesota

GENDER
Female

AGE
1

TYPE
Domestic shorthair
(torbie)

About

Pippin was born with a smol eye
and a wonky nose.

 **76/10**

PURRSONALITY
Pippin is the bestest-gurl ever.

NOSE
99/10

She really does
have the purrfect
wonky nose.

EYES

98/10

Pippin, stop
flirting with
me with that
winky eye.

*I'M SO SMITTEN
WITH THIS KITTEN!*

CATITUDE
"There will never
be another lady
like me. I purrfect."

110/10

MOUF

89/10

Ooh, that's the
sweetest smile.

Thursday

LOCATION

Nashville, Tennessee

GENDER

Female

AGE

1

TYPE

Domestic Longhair
(white with a gray spot)

About

Thursday is a fighter who is currently under observation after being diagnosed with FIP (Feline Infectious Peritonitis). She is also the cuddliest cat.

89/10

VOCALNESS

She meows with a Southern accent. "Yeehawmeow!"

88/10

FLOOFINESS

Cats do wear their fur bigger in the South.

SHE'S PRETTY AS A PEACH!

EARS

88/10

Thursday's curly ear floofs are enviable. Cats with straight ear floofs are thinking about perming theirs now.

MARKINGS

87/10

The gray spot really gives permanent bed head.

CHONKINESS 49/10
Squee! So squishy!

Livy

LOCATION
Lincoln, Nebraska

GENDER
Female

AGE
1

TYPE
Domestic medium hair
(black and white)

About

Livy was a feral kitten and lost her right eye from infection. Our cute little one-eyed kitty loves to sit like a human with her furry belly out.

EYES 49/10
This one-eyed pirate also doubles as a Jolly Roger flag.

BELLY 77/10
So nice to offer an open invitation to admire and feel that extra-squishy primordial pouch.

CATITUDE 43/10
"What do you mean I no hooman?"

VOCALNESS 79/10
"Yo Ho (A Pirate's Meow for Me)"

COLOR/MARKINGS 89/10
Livy's a superhero with that black cape.

Mushu

LOCATION
Lethbridge, Alberta

GENDER
Female

AGE
3

TYPE
Snowshoe Siamese
(chocolate point)

About

Mushu is a special-needs kitty rescued from an unethical breeder. She has stomatitis, hip dysplasia, and luxating patellas. She's pure joy and keeps us and our other two cats on our toes . . . lol.

EARS

55/10

Sung to the tune of the 1960s *Batman* theme song . . . "bat ears . . . bat ears."

FACE/TAIL

76/10

I'm always a fan of a color-coordinated kitty, and I love Mushu's matching face splotches and tail.

MARKINGS

99/10

Mushu is the purrfect patchwork kitty specimen.

PURRSONALITY

Mushu has the sweetest-ever factor.

38/10

SKILLZ

46/10

She spreads joy to everyone.

Wednesday

LOCATION

Rio, Wisconsin

GENDER

Female

AGE

3

TYPE

Domestic shorthair
(torbie)

About

Wednesday is a dwarf
cat, her back legs are
backward, and she
has hockey sticks for
front legs. In spite of all
that, she loves to play
and is hilarious.

CATITUDE
"Live. Laugh. Love."

97/10

118

98/10

PURRSONALITY
Wednesday is the sweetest angel ever.

87/10

SKILLZ
Hockey stick arms equal GOOOAAALLL!!!

LEGS
99/10
Wednesday has special, purrfect legs.

BELLY
98/10
Wednesday's low-rider belly drag will help keep those floors clean.

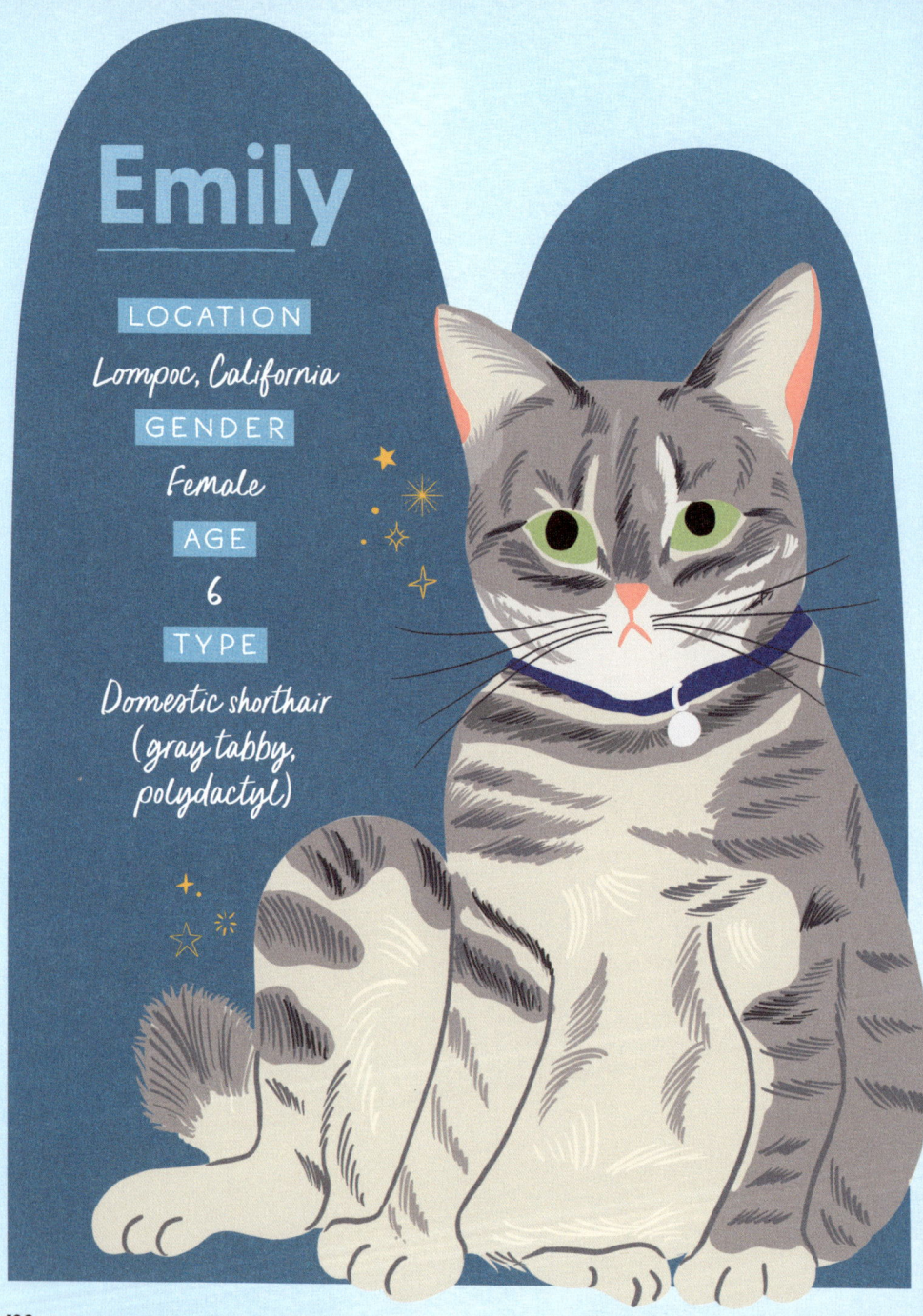

Emily

LOCATION

Lompoc, California

GENDER

Female

AGE

6

TYPE

Domestic shorthair
(gray tabby,
polydactyl)

About

Emily was my first foster kitten.
She has fought and won against FIP
and cancer. She is now a tripod kitty.

COLOR / MARKINGS
95/10
All hail this gray
tabby queen!

CATITUDE
87/10
"My illnesses don't
define me."

SKILLZ
99/10
She's the Bruce Lee
of cats, fighting FIP
and cancer!

TAKE THAT, FIP
AND CANCER!
POW!

FLOOFINESS
33/10
Emily is a living
plushie, soft
blanket, shag rug
... you name it.

PURRSONALITY
67/10
Emily is the purrfect
little lady.

Merle

LOCATION

Vancouver, Washington

GENDER

Male

AGE

7

TYPE

Domestic shorthair
(orange)

About

I rescued him as a baby, and he's my pet soulmate. It's been seven years and he's still waiting on that brain cell—maybe he'll use it to figure out the whole "depth perception" thing.

PURRSONALITY
88/10
I love a big orange goofball … or cheeseball?

COLOR
89/10
Ahoy, mateys! We've spotted an orange pirate boy. Arrrgh!

CALL ME CRAZY, BUT I DON'T HATE THE SMELL OF KITTY BREFS.

MOUF
66/10
Of course Merle has fishy brefs since he's a pirate!

CATITUDE
"Mom, I have idea. Wait, I forgots."
99/10

SKILLZ
78/10
Merle can touch his nose with his tongue.

Jameson Irish Whiskers

LOCATION

Newark, Delaware

GENDER

Male

AGE

7

TYPE

Domestic shorthair (black tuxedo)

TAIL

$88/10$

Jameson's superpower is an invisible tail.

About

Jameson was rescued from a major highway after being hit by a car and had to have a leg and his tail amputated. He loves to sing the songs of his people, and he is very handsome.

VOCALNESS

$94/10$

There's nothing more charming than a cat who meows with an Irish accent.

LEGS

99/10

Three leggies
are all one
needs!

CATITUDE

88/10

"I only need three
dress shoes to go
with my tuxedo."

49/10

POSE

I've never seen
a more joyful
pose. Ever.

London, England

GENDER

Male

AGE

8

TYPE

Domestic shorthair
(brown tabby
with white)

Patch

About

Patch is a rescue cat we rehomed with his mum, Martha, just over five years ago. Despite many health issues (epilepsy, kidney disease, and a heart murmur), he is a happy, loving, and sweet boy who loves nothing more than to snuggle up with his feline and human mums for hours on end. Well, he may love food even more than that . . .

CATITUDE
77/10
Hungry boi! "Mum, my bowl only half full."

SKILLZ
78/10
Patch loves to snoogle with felines and hoomans.

FACE
41/10
Patch is so emo with that hairstyle.

MOUF
67/10
The Kardashians are jealous of that pouty lower lip!

IN THIS SPECIAL CASE, I THINK PATCH SHOULD RECEIVE ALL MEALS IN BED. WHY DISRUPT ALL THAT LOVIN'?

MARKINGS
Extra-special tabbiness, including that lemur tail.
88/10

Misty

LOCATION
El Paso, Texas

GENDER
Female

AGE
9

TYPE
Korat (gray/silver)

About

Discarded in a shoebox at our veterinarian hospital on a cold
and rainy November weekend, Misty was cared for by our vets
until my daughter brought her home after taking our gray
tabby, Ned, for a checkup. She has a wonky hip and hops when
she runs. Her green eyes are a little crossed, and she doesn't
like loud sounds. One of a kind, she is perfectly beautiful.

FLOOFINESS
37/10
Misty always has the texture
of a freshly brushed coat.

LEGS
98/10
Bunny hoppin' is
much more fun
than cat walkin'.

EYES
88/10
"My crossed eyes
help me focus on
my foods."

CATITUDE
73/10
"I'm happy to not be
living in a shoebox."

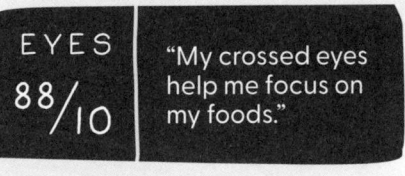

EARS
24/10
Her airplane ears
are noiseless, thank
goodness.

Zigford Johnston

LOCATION

Burlington, Ontario

GENDER

Male

AGE

10

TYPE

Domestic shorthair (black with a tiny spot of white on chest)

About

Zigford is blind, but he doesn't seem to mind because he starts purring as soon as someone speaks to him and all he wants to do is cuddle! He still plays even though he can't see, and we love him to bits!

COLOR/MARKINGS

93/10

Unlike the classic tuxedo cat, Zigford has opted for a black suit with a white string tie.

PURRSONALITY

99/10

Zigford has been declared the sweetest, floofiest little man.

CHONKINESS 87/10
We've got us the best big buddy boi.

CATITUDE

39/10

"Is someone there? Wanna cuddle?"

BELLY
59/10

You'll also get a stomach crease if you sit like this.

Gizmo

LOCATION

Oregon City, Oregon

GENDER

Male

AGE

13

TYPE

Domestic shorthair
(gray and white)

About

Gizmo is living his best life despite being diagnosed with hypertrophic cardiomyopathy two-and-a-half years ago. He thinks he's a baby and loves nothing more than being held like a baby. This super-sweet guy gets 12 out of 10 for therapeutic cuddles!

PURRSONLITY
88/10
He really has the best gray-and-white boi factor.

SKILLZ
87/10
Have you read Gizmo's book, *The Art of Snoogling*?

TEEFS
63/10
Gizmo is proud of those snagglers, and rightfully so!

#1 CAT TIMES BEST SELLER!

POSE
75/10
Not only does Gizmo like to be held like a bebe but he also likes to sleep like a bebe.

CATITUDE
Eepiness! "I need my beauty rest, hoomans."
49/10

Dorito

LOCATION

Newark, New Jersey

GENDER

Male

AGE

14

TYPE

Domestic shorthair (brown tabby with white)

About

This lil' chip was rescued from an abusive home when he was six months old and has been fighting to live his best life ever since. Battling back from upper respiratory issues (which resulted in the cutest snore and most unique purr!) and FIV (Feline Immunodeficiency Virus) during kittenhood to losing most of his teeth and developing a slight kidney issue in old age, Dorito takes his job as the family's furry alarm clock seriously, keeping everyone on schedule for morning and nighttime routines, but always finding moments each day to stretch out in a sunbeam.

CATITUDE 100/10
"Live life to the fullest. Always!"

MARKINGS

84/10

Those purrfect tabby swirls are making me very, very sleepy . . .

SKILLZ

77/10

Being the family alarm clock is a huge responsibility. The Swiss could probably learn a thing or two from Dorito.

THIS HAS BEEN CONFIRMED BY HIS MOM!

PURRSONALITY

57/10

Dorito definitely likes to slink out of uncomfortable situations.

44/10

FACE

I just want to give that sweet white chin some scratchies.

Raúl

LOCATION

Porto, Portugal

GENDER

Male

AGE

15

TYPE

Domestic shorthair
(brown tabby)

About

Raúl is a very shy lovebug who spoons me even on the hottest summer days. Aside from his age, he's also on palliative care for gastric lymphoma and responding very well to it. He's being a fantastic trooper.

PURRSONALITY

Raúl has the sweetest shy-boi factor.

99/10

CATITUDE
999/10
Watch out, Ronaldo! Raúl is waiting in the wings to be Portugal's sweetheart.

PEETS
89/10
I love those purrfect lion paws.

MARKINGS
99/10
Raúl's tabby M stands for Meowgnificent.

99/10

SKILLZ
A cat who spoons a hooman? Sign me up!

Linus

LOCATION

San Clemente, California

GENDER

Male

AGE

16

TYPE

Domestic shorthair
(orange tabby with white)

About

The sweetest little miracle boi, Linus is a fighter. He was diagnosed with hypertrophic cardiomyopathy and congestive heart failure five years ago and got through saddle thrombus two-and-a-half years ago, and though he has renal disease, episodes of kidney infection, and severe anemia this year, he is still going strong. He is so affectionate and gives tons of kisses.

EYES

65/10

"I winz all staring contests."

POSE

88/10

As you can see (opposite), Linus is the strongest, chillest boi.

99/10

PURRSONALITY

Linus is the sweetest orange man ever.

Wall of Feline Fame

ANGEL 62

BEAN 56

BELLA 36

BRANDI 68

BRUNSWICK 48

BUBBLES 88

BUDDY "THE ELF" EDENS 30

CARAMEL 78

CARMINE 72

CHESTER 38

CHINA 106

CHRISSIE 34

CJ AND COCO 86

DAVE 82

DORITO 134

EDIE 92

EMILY 120

EMMA 28

FELIX 16

FREDDIE PURR-CURRY 26

GANYMEDE 60

GIZMO 132

JACK 20

JAMESON IRISH WHISKERS 124

LINUS 138

LITTLE T 80

LIVY 114

LUMI AND HINOKI 118

LUNA 40

MARCO 84

MERLE 122

MILO HUCKLEBERRY VENTIMIGLIO 54

MISTY 128

MUFFIN 64

MUSHU 116

NEESHA 98

NEWTON (NEWT) 32

OZZIE 58

PATCH 126

PEPPER 96

PEPPERRICKA (PEPPER) 104

PINKY 52

PIPPIN 110

PRINCESS LEIA 50

RASHIDA LEOPARDS (ZOEY) 70

RAÚL 136

REX 100

ROMEO (MOMO) 90

SAFFRON 46

SELMA 102

SIMBA 74

SKYE BLUE HUMPHREY BOGART (BOGIE) 66

TAFFY THE BOARDWALK CAT 42

THURSDAY 112

TUESDAY 94

VIOLET 14

WEDNESDAY 118

XAVIER 22

YZMA 24

ZIGFORD JOHNSTON 130

Acknowledgments

This book would not be possible without all the amazing cat parents—over six hundred!—who sent in pictures and loving descriptions of their cats for a chance to be in our book. We loved every single one of your cats and had the hardest time narrowing them down to the ones featured. We appreciate you as well as all the millions of people who follow along on our adventures on social media. One thing that is certain: There is always a need for more cat videos!

I would like to thank my wife and family for their support with all my crazy ideas and for being such kind and caring humans. I'm proud to say that all of you recognize the way that animals can make our lives better. Finally, I want to thank Erin Canning and the team at The Quarto Group for realizing the world needed this book and my manager, Ashley Koll, for helping me connect with more and more people.

About the Author

Matthew McGlasson has been a veterinarian and leader in the animal health industry for over twenty years. He has witnessed first-hand the life-changing power of the human-animal bond. Dr. McGlasson has been featured in numerous professional journals and publications, and he is a frequent speaker at national veterinary conferences. In 2022, he was awarded the Veterinary Hero Award presented by DVM360. When his daughter created a TikTok account for him in 2020, he had no idea that his videos would reach millions and millions of people.

Dr. McGlasson is "that guy," you know, the one whom his neighbors whisper about because he pushes his cats around the neighborhood in strollers. He lives in Fort Mitchell, Kentucky, with his beautiful wife, four children, four cats, and three dogs. Three of the McGlasson's kittles (Rupaul, Rushie, and Princess Baby Nugget Wobbles the First) have special needs and are currently living their best lives.

First published in 2025 by Rock Point,
an imprint of The Quarto Group,
142 West 36th Street, 4th Floor,
New York, NY 10018, USA
T (212) 779-4972
www.Quarto.com

Rock Point titles are also available
at discount for retail, wholesale,
promotional and bulk purchase.
For details, contact the Special
Sales Manager by email at
specialsales@quarto.com or
by mail at The Quarto Group,
Attn: Special Sales Manager,
100 Cummings Center Suite,
265D, Beverly, MA 01915, USA.

10 9 8 7 6 5 4 3 2 1

ISBN: 978-1-57715-492-1

Digital edition published in 2025
eISBN: 978-0-7603-9373-4

Library of Congress Cataloging-in-
Publication Data available upon request.

Publisher: Rage Kindelsperger
Creative Director: Laura Drew
Senior Art Director: Marisa Kwek
Editorial Director: Erin Canning
Managing Editor: Cara Donaldson
Cover and Interior Design: Madeleine Kane
Illustrations: Ayang Cempaka

Printed in China